I simply love this booklet! There  to the horror of sexual abuse: T to just get over it; or they may exaggerate it, sending sufferers on a lifelong and futile journey of introspection. Or they can point them to the good news that there is a Suffering Savior who loves, welcomes, completely understands, and restores victims. Bob Kellemen knows this good news and the Suffering Savior well. He knows also how to bring the brokenhearted into contact with the living Christ who loves and heals. What a wonderful help *Sexual Abuse: Beauty for Ashes* is!

> —**Elyse Fitzpatrick,** counselor with the Institute for Biblical Counseling and Discipleship

With biblical wisdom and pastoral sensitivity, Kelleman offers a redemptive vision and pathway in the aftermath of sexual abuse—first by exposing Satan's attempt to destroy faith, hope, peace, and love through the wickedness of sexual abuse, then by showing how our Redeemer overcomes evil by his transforming grace. *Sexual Abuse: Beauty for Ashes* is a great resource to help the church care for one another with the compassionate and powerful realities of the gospel.

> —**Robert K. Cheong,** pastor of care, Sojourn Community Church

The path to healing from the damage of sexual abuse is murky and often lonely for those who walk it. Vistas that reveal progress are rare. Too often the spiritual advice and care victims receive ends up being simplistic or absent. Using an extended case study, Dr. Kellemen provides a realistic and hope-filled roadmap to guide pastors, loved ones, and victims as they explore the damage done by sexual abuse and the journey to renewed vitality. Like actual maps, this booklet may be small, but it contains depth rarely seen in Christian treatments of sexual abuse recovery.

> —**Philip G. Monroe,** professor of counseling and psychology, Biblical Seminary; director of Global Trauma Recovery Institute

This booklet will transform heaps of sackcloth and ashes into rows of beautiful garments. Bob skillfully weaves together Tamar's ancient agony with Ashley's modern misery to produce a tapestry of suffering and sin ready to receive the precious threads of our Savior's sympathy, support, and salvation.

> —**David Murray,** author of *Christians Get Depressed Too*

The booklet you hold in your hand is a wonderfully gentle blend of the grace and truth found only in Jesus Christ. Whether you are the victim of sexual abuse or a loving friend who wants to minister God's hope to those who have had their hope stolen, you will find the biblical counsel here a great help and encouragement.

—**Paul Tautges,** pastor of Immanuel Bible Church; founder of the *Counseling One Another* blog

Dr. Kellemen's gospel insights are for both the sexually abused and the pastor. For the person who was abused, you will find a clear and caring path and will notice that you are already on it. This will give you hope. For the pastor, the scope of sexual abuse is such that you will be preaching on it, and this booklet opens the story of Tamar in such a way that your sermon series is ready to go with a gospel-centered foundation.

—**Ed Welch,** faculty member of the Christian Counseling and Educational Foundation; author of *Shame Interrupted*

If you have ever been a victim of sexual abuse, please read this vital booklet. You will experience so much care, so much compassion, so much Scripture, and so much of the good news of the gospel. If you are a pastor or counselor, please read it and learn how to extend that same care, compassion, Scripture, and gospel grace to others. Here is the gospel applied carefully and tenderly to real life.

—**Tim Challies,** pastor of Grace Fellowship Church; author of *The Next Story*

There is an epidemic of sexual abuse, and victims need the kind of hope and healing that only the gospel of Jesus Christ provides. Tragically, most churches and Christians are woefully unprepared to help those who have been abused sexually. In this booklet Dr. Kellemen offers clear, accessible, gospel-based help for the many victims of sexual abuse and teaches us all how to face sexual abuse side by side with Christ.

—**Justin and Lindsey Holcomb,** authors of *Rid of My Disgrace: Hope and Healing for Victims of Sexual Assault*

Sexual Abuse

The GOSPEL for REAL LIFE series

Abuse: Finding Hope in Christ
Anxiety: Anatomy and Cure
Borderline Personality: A Scriptural Perspective
Burnout: Resting in God's Fairness
Cutting: A Healing Response
Depression: The Sun Always Rises
God's Attributes: Rest for Life's Struggles
Post-Traumatic Stress Disorder: Recovering Hope
Sexual Abuse: Beauty for Ashes
Vulnerability: Blessing in the Beatitudes

Brad Hambrick, Series Editor

Sexual Abuse

BEAUTY FOR ASHES

ROBERT W. KELLEMEN

P&R
PUBLISHING
P.O. BOX 817 • PHILLIPSBURG • NEW JERSEY 08865-0817

ISBN: 978-1-59638-419-4 (pbk)
ISBN: 978-1-59638-621-1 (ePub)
ISBN: 978-1-59638-622-8 (Mobi)

Printed in the United States of America

I T WAS THE DAY AFTER their twin sons' eleventh birthday that Ashley and her husband, Nate, came to see me at church. Ashley, with trembling voice, shaking hands, and tears streaming down her face, shared with me that twenty-five years earlier, not long after her eleventh birthday, a relative had begun sexually abusing her.

Those who knew Ashley would have been shocked. She grew up in a churchgoing home, actively served at church as an adult, served as a group leader in the women's ministry, and was always "pleasant."

As Ashley described herself, "Yes, I'm the good girl from the good home. The good mom, the good wife. But nobody knows the ugliness I feel inside me. Nobody knows how I've pretended and denied all these years. And I just can't keep faking it any longer. Inside, I'm a mess. Depressed to the point that at times I've thought of suicide. Always fearful and anxious—terrified I'll displease someone. Terrified someone will find out what an empty but evil thing I am . . ."

As Ashley's voice trailed off, Nate asked, "Pastor Bob, can you help? Does the Bible offer any hope for my wife?"

GRACE FOR OUR DISGRACE

Nate's questions are likely your questions. "Can the church help those who have been sexually abused? Does Christianity, the gospel, God's Word, offer hope for those who have experienced the horrors of sexual abuse?" You may ask because you're a "people helper." You may ask because someone you love has been abused and you feel helpless. You may ask because you're a sexual abuse "survivor," but you don't feel like you're surviving much at all.

Nate's questions are fair questions, especially since the church seems to be in as much denial as some abuse victims. Recently, while speaking before a group of more than one hundred pastors, I asked how many had preached on sexual, physical, or emotional abuse in the past five years. Not one hand went up. I asked how many had received any training in Bible college or seminary to assist them in ministering to sexual abuse victims. Again, not a single hand shot up. I asked how many had ever preached on 2 Samuel 13 or any of the "texts of terror" passages (especially those in Genesis that address the abuse of women). Only four men had ever done so, and all four acknowledged that they never related the message to the issue of sexual abuse. Many of the pastors even admitted that when preaching through Genesis or 2 Samuel, they purpose-fully skipped the texts of terror passages.

Sexual abuse ravages the soul. It causes unimaginable distress, damage, and disgrace. It is faced honestly and openly in the Bible. Yet we either mistreat it or ignore it. This is to our shame. It is time for a change.

In this booklet we want to learn how to face sexual abuse face-to-face with Christ. We want to understand how the Evil One attempts to use sexual abuse to destroy faith, hope, peace, and love. We want to obtain wise counsel from the Divine Counselor through his Word, which teaches us that *grace is God's prescription for the disgrace of sexual abuse.* Specifically, we want to journey together on God's pathway from *loss of trust* to *faith,* from *powerlessness* to *hope,* from *shame* to *shalom and peace,* and from *being used and feeling useless* to *love.*

Before we begin, I want to share a personal word to those who have been sexually abused. I know you wonder if the shattered pieces of your life can be reassembled. I know you long for compassionate wisdom for moving from victim to victor in Christ. In what you're about to read, I want to walk with you through 2 Samuel 13 on a journey with Tamar—a woman who endured sexual abuse at the hands of her half-brother. With Tamar we will learn how to apply gospel truth to our lives so we can experience four living examples of the truth that states that where sin abounds, grace superabounds. Together, we'll experience (1) sustaining faith that preserves trust in the midst of doubt, (2) healing hope that clings to the goodness of God in the midst of the badness of life, (3) reconciling peace that receives Christ's grace in the midst of our disgrace, and (4) guiding love that offers beauty in the midst of ashes.

GOD'S CENTRAL MESSAGE TO YOU

While we'll focus primarily on one passage (2 Sam. 13), we need to place that passage within the larger framework of the overriding purpose of the Bible. Let's frame it together by considering God's central message to you.

God's Mission Statement

Today we hear all about "mission statements." Businesses have them, churches develop them, even families and individuals craft mission statements. What is God's mission statement? What is the central message that God wants to communicate to you as you read his Word?

I'm sure we could each craft unique responses to that question. Here's my three-word summary of God's mission statement:

"I Am Indispensable."

Paul's words in 2 Corinthians 1:8–9 communicate this message. "We were under great pressure, far beyond our ability to endure, so that we despaired even of life. Indeed, in our hearts we felt the sentence of death. But this happened *that we might not rely on ourselves but on God, who raises the dead."*

In Bryan Chapell's *Christ-Centered Preaching*, he urges us to find the FCF—Fallen Condition Focus—in every passage.[1] All of Scripture encourages us to shout, like the elderly woman in those old commercials, "Help! I've fallen and I can't get up!" The consistent message of every biblical text is that *we desperately need God.* The Bible is the most honest, realistic, earthy book ever written. God's Word is not an advertisement for a trouble-free life. Instead, it advertises our need for God's grace because of our continual struggle with suffering and sin.

God says to us, "You are hopeless and helpless without my grace. I offer it to you in my Son. You cannot survive your suffering or overcome your sin apart from my grace. I am indispensable."

The Central Message of Life and of Ministry

As we attempt to minister to one another, we can translate this central message of the Bible into a statement about the central message of life lived in a fallen world.

> *One-another ministry is defective unless we apply Christ's grace to deal both with the evils we have suffered and with the sins we have committed.*

We are *coram Deo* beings. That is, God designed us to live face-to-face in his presence. We are also *sola gratia* beings—God designed us to live by grace alone. Therefore, the essence of our life together is to encourage one another to live face-to-face with God through grace as we face suffering and fight against sin. We want to create in one another a greater awareness of God so that Christ and his grace permeate how we live each

1. Bryan Chapell, *Christ-Centered Preaching: Redeeming the Expository Sermon*, 2nd ed. (Grand Rapids: Baker Academics, 2005).

day. Here's how I summarize it when I'm teaching on biblical counseling and spiritual friendship:

Dealing with Suffering: God Is Good Even When Life Is Bad

Dealing with Sinning: God Is Gracious Even When I Am Sinful

The Central Message of 2 Samuel 9 to 1 Kings 2

God's indispensability is exactly the message of the life of David, especially from 2 Samuel 9 to 1 Kings 2. Here we have David, a man after God's own heart. David, God's chosen servant. David, the recipient of God's covenant promises. David, the man whose life is a *mess—filled with sin and suffering.* In this section of Scripture, David commits adultery, lies, murders, does nothing when his son rapes his daughter, and is ousted from the throne of Israel by another son. If any section of the Bible was written to show us that *we need God,* this is it. The entire Davidic narrative points us to our ultimate need for the Greater David—for Jesus Christ.

This narrative points us to our need for our gracious and faithful God. David and his family suffer tragedy after tragedy, and through it all God remains eternally faithful to his promises. David and his family sin time after time, and God forgives time after time. God will not cast off David, nor will he cast off you or me. The message of the Bible, the message of life and ministry, the message of 2 Samuel 9 to 1 Kings 2, and the message of 2 Samuel 13 are all the same—*grace is God's prescription for our disgrace.* Grace is God's medicine of choice for our suffering and sin.

UNDERSTANDING THE DAMAGE DONE BY SEXUAL ABUSE: 2 SAMUEL 13

In looking to 2 Samuel 13, I am *not* implying that this one passage has all the wisdom we need to address this complex and painful issue. Perhaps a little personal history will help to place this passage into perspective. When I teach a semester-long seminary class on sexual abuse recovery, I start by telling my students that "God dragged me kicking and screaming into a focus on sexual abuse counseling." By that, I do not imply a lack of compassion for those who have been sexually abused. I'm stating the opposite. I feel deeply for those who have been sexually abused. So deeply that, especially at first, counseling abuse victims was overwhelming for me.

I vividly remember the first sexual abuse survivor I worked with—Tim. Initially, I felt clueless to help Tim. He educated me as much as I counseled him—helping me to understand the damage done by and the dynamics related to sexual abuse. In seeking to minister to Tim, I turned to another source—the Bible—examining it literally cover to cover to see what it teaches about sexual abuse and sexual abuse recovery. Through that process I've come to see that God's Word provides us with robust, relevant, relational wisdom for addressing the horrors of sexual abuse.

Tamar's narrative in 2 Samuel 13 is part of that larger biblical portrait of sexual abuse and sexual abuse recovery. It remark-ably represents themes woven throughout the rest of Scripture's teaching on sexual abuse—the damage done and the path to God's healing hope.

Why Examine the Damage Done?

During my three decades of ministry as a biblical counselor, I've become convinced that we need to develop a biblical "sufferology"—a biblical theology of and perspective on suffering and healing. The Bible is brimming with it. We can hardly open a single page and not see God addressing suffering.[2] If we are to be truly biblical

2. For my development of a biblical model of "sufferology," see Robert Kellemen, *God's Healing for Life's Losses: How to Find Hope for the Hurting* (Winona Lake, IN: BMH Books, 2010).

counselors and one-another ministers, then we must examine the damage done to the souls of those who have suffered sexual abuse.

We also need a clear picture of the prime strategy of the Evil One. The Prince of Darkness is our most radical enemy. It is his strategy to use the horrors of sexual abuse to attempt to destroy that which enables us to be most human: faith, hope, peace, and love. To win the battle in Christ, through Christ, and by Christ, we must first name the damage that has been done to us as bearers of the image of God.

OUR JOURNEY IN: COMPASS POINTS OF THE SOUL

God has not left us clueless. Throughout the Bible, including in 2 Samuel 13, God lays before us what we need to know to grasp the primary damage of sexual abuse. The Bible teaches us that sexual abuse is ultimately spiritual abuse—it attacks us body *and* soul.

In Tamar's life we see this damage, this attempted destruction, in four primary ways. As we explore Tamar's narrative, we'll use the language of a "journey." This allows her story to show us four road map markers, four compass points, on the *journey into the soul* of a person who has been sexually abused. This helps us to avoid the idea of "stages" or "phases," which might mistakenly cause us to think that there exists some common, linear, nice and neat process. There's nothing nice or neat about sexual abuse! It is evil and complex, awful and hideous. Each situation is different, and each victim of abuse is a unique image bearer. Yet we can detect some themes that occur across Scripture and across the lives and souls of those who have been abused. We will consider four such themes from 2 Samuel 13.

Journey One: The Damage of Loss of Trust—The Attempted Destruction of Faith (2 Sam. 13:1–12)

Amnon is King David's firstborn, the heir apparent to the throne. He also happens to be the stepbrother of the beautiful

Tamar. And he happens to be in love with her, or so he says—
God labels Amnon's feelings incestuous lust. His unbridled lusts
and his unfulfilled longings are eating him alive until his shrewd
friend, Jonadab, schemes up a plan to get Amnon alone with
Tamar.

Pretending to be ill, Amnon tells Daddy, King David, that
he would like to have his sister Tamar bring him some food.
David becomes the unwitting go-between, sending his daughter
into the lion's den with his son. Innocently, naively, and lovingly,
Tamar prepares a feast fit for a king-to-be. Amnon, according to
plan, refuses to eat and sends everyone out of the room.

We pick up the story at 2 Samuel 13:10–12.

> Then Amnon said to Tamar, "Bring the food here into my
> bedroom so I may eat from your hand." And Tamar took the
> bread she had prepared and brought it to her brother Amnon
> in his bedroom. But when she took it to him to eat, he grabbed
> her and said, "Come to bed with me, my sister."
>
> "Don't, my brother!" she said to him.

Here we witness the damage of loss of trust. Did you catch
the phrases "my sister" and "my brother"? In fact, the inspired
narrator repeatedly emphasizes that *this is family!* Twenty times
in the Hebrew of 13:1–22 we read of family ties: son of, sister of,
your brother, your father. The very person who should protect
and cherish Tamar violates her instead. Amnon uses Tamar's
untainted trust as a doorway to gain access to her body and
soul. She opens her heart to her father and brother only to have
it betrayed and crushed.

Satan is shrewd. He knows that God built us to trust him.
He also knows that because of the fall, our inclination is to trust
ourselves or anyone and anything but God. So Satan loves to
feed our distrust of God with *betrayal by those who ought to be
trustworthy.* He wants faith to look foolish.

Can you picture it? God is wooing us back to himself, drawing us home to his holy and loving heart, to Christ our faithful Savior. All the while Satan is whispering, "You can't trust him. You can't trust anyone. You can't even trust *family!* Don't be foolish. Trust only yourself!" Evil wins the battle for our soul to the extent that we experience trust in others and in God as dangerous and foolish.

Sexual abuse, especially incestuous sexual abuse—abuse by a relative—shrinks the heart, shrivels the soul. Ashley's description depicts this powerfully. "I responded to my abuse by erecting a wall around my heart so that I could close the door of trust to God and others. I picture myself slamming the door shut, double-bolting it, bracing my shoulder against it, and trying with all my might to keep God and everybody else out." She concluded that it was unsafe to open her soul to anyone . . . including God.

In this, Ashley is much like Tamar. In 13:13 she speaks of her "disgrace," and in 13:20 the text describes her as "desolate." (We'll examine both words in more detail later.) Both Hebrew words speak of *relational struggle*: alienation from God, separation from others, and dis-integration from self. Sexual abuse is *relational* abuse that seeks to sever our capacity for mutual connection.

Journey Two: The Damage of Powerlessness—The Attempted Destruction of Hope (2 Sam. 13:2, 11–14)

Satan attempts to destroy faith by the damage of loss of trust, and he attempts to destroy hope by the damage of loss of power. The narrator informs us that the male, Amnon, begins powerless—he's frustrated because it seems impossible for him to get what he wants. The female, Tamar, begins pure, at peace, and protected—she is the beautiful virgin daughter of the king.

And then the shift occurs. Tamar endures the titanic sinking of everything she had ever known and hoped for.

We read in 13:11 that Amnon "grabbed her." The Hebrew word pictures laying hold of, seizing, clutching. The author is informing us that this was a violent act of rape. This was a ruthless exercise of power by a man playing God with a woman's life.

Fighting against Amnon, Tamar cries out in 13:12, "Don't force me." She attempts to retain her voice and reclaim her power. In the Hebrew, Tamar speaks one powerful vocative word: "No!" She then confronts her attacker. "You would be like one of the wicked fools in Israel" (13:13).

Ignoring her and thinking only of his lusts, Amnon leaves Tamar voiceless and powerless. "But he refused to listen to her, and since he was stronger than she, he raped her" (13:14). He forces himself upon her. "Force" (13:12) means to oppress, humiliate, violate, and abuse. The Old Testament uses the word several times for forced intercourse, violent intrusion— rape. It pictures the victim so intimidated that she cowers in a corner. This is a cruel act of a powerful person overpowering the weak.

Ashley described her sense of powerlessness, helplessness, and hopelessness. "While people think I'm oh-so-pleasant, kind, sweet, and nice, the truth is that I live by the motto: 'Why bother? Why want? Why care?' I feel better when I feel numb. I look nice because I never exert myself because it's just not worth it. It only hurts to hope, hurts to dream."

Ashley told me about going to see the musical *Les Misérables* with Nate. The character she identified with the most was Fantine and the death of hope Fantine's soul endured. Abandoned by the father of her child and now near death, Fantine looks back on life with regret and looks ahead with hopelessness. She is a picture of what happens when we lose sight of God in the midst of life's losses and abuses.

Ashley related to her own life the despairing words of Fantine's song, "I Dreamed a Dream": "Like Fantine, once I was young and dreamed grand dreams, but my dreams were dashed and my hope torn to shreds. Like her, my dreams have died and I don't have the strength to weather the storms of life anymore. All my dreams have turned to shame."

These are words that Satan loves to hear. They are the words often on the lips of the sexual abuse victim. "Now life has killed the dream I dreamed."[3] These are the words of a Christian who has lost sight of Christ. The sexual abuse victim who despairs of hope does not cry out with the psalmist, "I will lift up mine eyes unto the hills, from whence cometh my help" (Ps. 121:1 KJV). The despairing sexual abuse victim refuses to believe that help will ever come for a powerless and voiceless person like herself. As Ashley put it, "Life is empty today, and it will never change, only get worse."

Journey Three: The Damage of Shame—The Attempted Destruction of Peace/Shalom (2 Sam. 13:13–17)

The end result of the loss of faith and hope is shame. Tamar verbalizes her shame in 13:13. "What about me? Where could I get rid of my disgrace?" Do you hear the desperation in her voice? She feels surrounded by disgrace. Wherever she goes she feels as if all eyes are on her—that everyone knows. And she feels as if there is no place of grace that can remedy her disgrace.

The Hebrew language maintains a twofold use of the word *disgrace*, and both fit the context of sexual abuse. The first use means to feel contempt for oneself, to feel reproach, to feel guilty and filthy. Many sexual abuse victims feel a tremendous amount of false guilt that leads to a sense of worthlessness and soul ugliness.

One way that Ashley conveyed her sense of ugliness and shame was by her inability to make eye contact. She referenced another scene in *Les Misérables*—the opening scene where the convict Jean Valjean and other prisoners are working like slaves.

3. Herbert Kretzmer, "I Dreamed a Dream," *Les Misérables* (Milwaukee: Hal Leonard Corporation, 1987).

Treated as subhuman, they're singing, "Look down, look down! Don't look 'em in the eye."[4]

Ashley explained. "That's how I feel—so ashamed. I'm convinced that people's eyes can pierce right into my soul and see the pit of evil that I and everyone else want to reject. And though I know it's not true, some days I even wonder if Jesus cares." Instead of being an open recipient of grace, Ashley felt like a black hole of disgrace.

A sexual abuser like Amnon takes delight when his victim feels guilty. This coincides with the second Hebrew use of this word "disgrace"—casting blame on and imputing guilt to another person. We see this clearly in 13:17. "He called his personal servant and said, 'Get this woman out of here and bolt the door after her.'" By putting her out and sending her away, Amnon shouts the message that she had shamefully approached him and that she was guilty of disgraceful conduct and attempted seduction. He bolts the door as if her femininity is dangerous. Amnon's actions are clearly designed to paint Tamar as a filthy harlot.

It is chillingly like the modern-day horror stories of the abuser who attempts to silence his victim with lies like, "Your parents won't want you if they find out what *you* did." "Your mom would stop loving you and give you up for adoption." "The police would arrest *you* for this."

The combined impact of self-contempt and imputed shame partially explains some of the symptoms that Ashley was experiencing. She struggled with chronic low-grade depression and joylessness, which at times turned into full-blown depression and suicidal ideations. She reported that she never enjoyed sex and, in fact, never enjoyed any pleasures. While others saw her as so "together," she often secretly felt like she was "coming unglued, falling apart, near a breakdown." While others appreciated her

---

4. Kretzmer, "Work Song," *Les Misérables*.

kind spirit, she would say, "I don't even know this person they're describing. I'm a stranger to myself." And " 'Kindness'? That's just because I'm terrified of anyone ever rejecting me. I'm the stereotypical perfectionistic people-pleaser."

All of these symptoms reflect the opposite of peace, of biblical shalom. Shalom is much more than the absence of enmity or the cessation of warfare. Shalom is the active, calming presence of harmony—relational harmony. Shalom with God conquers alienation and involves reconciliation and the confidence that through Christ we are accepted in the beloved. Shalom with others conquers separation and involves connection and the confidence that mutual sacrificial love is possible and desirable. Shalom with self conquers dis-integration and involves integration and confidence regarding our identity in Christ and a sense of personal wholeness.

Journey Four: The Damage of Being Used and Feeling Useless—The Attempted Destruction of Love (2 Sam. 13:14–20)

Satan heaps damage on top of damage. In 2 Samuel 13:14, the inspired narrator exposes the damage of being used and feeling useless—the attempted destruction of love. "He raped her." The Hebrew is brutal. It pictures her lifeless, stiff as a board, frozen like a statue, and left for dead.

Amnon used her and then rejected her. "Then Amnon hated her with intense hatred. In fact, he hated her more than he had loved her. Amnon said to her, 'Get up and get out!' " (13:15). Tamar was used and then abused. She was first regarded, then discarded. Amnon knew nothing about true love. Amnon the rapist, the sexual abuser, is filled with selfishness, acting in unprincipled, self-indulgent self-interest. What Amnon experienced was lust, not love. He gratified his animal passions and then humiliated her further by casting her off like a filthy rag.[5]

---

5. See C. F. Keil and F. Delitzsch, *Commentary on the Old Testament: Volume II—Joshua, Judges, Ruth, I & II Samuel* (Grand Rapids: Eerdmans, 1980), 399.

He dehumanizes her. Our modern translations are too polite. "Get this woman out of here and bolt the door after her." The word "woman" is not in the Hebrew. It is literally, "Get *this* out of here." Tamar went from being the king's daughter and the king-to-be's sister to being a *thing*. "Get *this thing* out of here!" She is nameless—nothing more than an object; that is, disposable trash.

In so doing, Amnon condemns Tamar to a life sentence of desolation. And she realizes it. Her symbolic actions in 13:18–19 portray how she felt that every shred of dignity had been ripped away. "So his servant put her out and bolted the door after her. She was wearing a richly ornamented robe, for this was the kind of garment the virgin daughters of the king wore. Tamar put ashes on her head and tore the ornamented robe she was wearing."

No one else looks upon her with love and respect, but the inspired narrator forces us to look at Tamar. God sees. And Tamar sees—she sees her clothes that had proclaimed her royalty and her purity. And she shreds them as Amnon had shredded her.

Matthew Henry insightfully explains that in shedding her virginal clothes, Tamar expresses her loathing for her own beauty and femininity because they had occasioned Amnon's unlawful lust.[6] Sexual abuse is not only physical abuse; it is not only spiritual abuse; it is not only relational abuse; it is also *gender* abuse. God created us as female image bearers or male image bearers. We are female or male not only in our bodies, but also in the essence of our souls, our selves, our personhood. Sexual abuse abuses a female soul and body or a male soul and body.

The results are clear and formidable. Tamar lays aside her royal ornaments and retires into a lonely and private existence ever after. Her lot in life is not "happy ever after,"

6. Matthew Henry, *The Matthew Henry Commentary* (Grand Rapids: Zondervan, 1961), 344.

but "lonely and loveless ever after." "And Tamar lived in her brother Absalom's house, a desolate woman" (13:20). As Matthew Henry summarizes, "She lived in solitude and sorrow."[7] Evil's most scurrilous work is in destroying our passion to love. Evil destroys love by causing us to feel ashamed of our desire to be loved and to love.

As Ashley, Nate, and I discussed Tamar's story together, Ashley explained, "I can so relate to Tamar. She's tearing her robes in grief and lament because her heart has been torn. It's like she's saying, 'I'm ruined for love—loveless and worthless. I'm no longer a loved, worthy child of the King. I'm taking off the King's garments. I'm now useless for the kingdom. Oh, I'll make it to heaven, but I'll have nothing to offer my King because my soul has nothing to offer anyone.' I know it's a lie, but I find myself believing it nonetheless."

Our adversary, the Devil, uses sexual abuse to put a chokehold on our redeemed spirit. I imagine him saying, "All right, God, if heaven is yours, then I want the earth. And if the earth is yours, then I want to ruin it. And if you promise to keep their souls forever, then I want to pummel their spirits." The Christian who has been sexually abused, and who succumbs to Satan's lies, feels used and useless—unable to love and be loved.

PAINTING PORTRAITS OF THE DAMAGE DONE

Putting it all together, we can suggest four summary pictures that help to frame (but certainly not to understand fully) some of the horrific damage done by sexual abuse.

1. The Loss of *Faith*: The Door of the Heart Bolted Shut
2. The Loss of *Hope*: The Death of Dreams—"Life Has Killed the Dream I Dreamed"

7. Ibid.

3. The Loss of *Peace*: The Downcast Eyes—"Look Down! Look Down!"
4. The Loss of *Love*: The Torn Robes of the King's Child

These four images convey and capture four "black holes" of emptiness that often result from sexual abuse. We now address how the gospel of Christ's grace shines the light of the Son into these black holes.

FROM VICTIM TO VICTOR IN CHRIST: BEAUTY FOR ASHES

I understand that some people do not appreciate or accept the "victim" terminology. If by *victim* one means an ongoing victimization mentality of helplessness and hopelessness, then I would not choose that word either. However, I fear that sometimes we minimize the horrible sinfulness of abuse and the profound consequences of abuse when we reject the truth that the person who was abused *was victimized*. Sexual abuse has a perpetrator *and* a victim. We've witnessed some results of this victimization in the biblical narrative of Tamar and in the personal narrative of Ashley.

God's Word does not pretend. It presents a real and raw picture of the damage done in the life of the sexual abuse victim. At the same time, God's Word offers authoritative, sufficient, relevant, and profound wisdom for the ongoing journey from victim to victor in Christ.

Of course, even the word *victory* can be misunderstood and misapplied. Victory does not mean the memories are wiped away. Victory does not mean that all emotions are changed with the snap of a finger or the quoting of a verse. Instead, victory involves a lifelong journey with Christ and the body of Christ.

THE JOURNEY OUT: THE PATHWAY TO GOD'S HEALING HOPE

To summarize that journey, I'll use a biblical approach to Christian care that has been developed throughout two thousand years of church history.[8]

- *Sustaining*: It's Normal to Hurt
- *Healing*: It's Possible to Hope
- *Reconciling*: It's Horrible to Sin, but Wonderful to Be Forgiven
- *Guiding*: It's Supernatural to Mature

We'll take this general "map" of historic Christian care and apply it specifically to healing from the four primary areas of damage caused by sexual abuse.

1. Journey One: Sustaining Faith—Preserving Trust in the Midst of Doubt
2. Journey Two: Healing Hope—Clinging to the Goodness of God in the Midst of the Badness of Life
3. Journey Three: Reconciling Peace—Receiving Christ's Grace in the Midst of Our Disgrace
4. Journey Four: Guiding Love—Offering Beauty in the Midst of Ashes

As we explore these four aspects of the healing journey, we'll use my biblical counseling with Ashley as an example. In this way we can illustrate the application of biblical principles both for the victim of abuse and for the person helping the abuse victim.

8. For a fuller development of this biblical and historical approach, see Robert Kellemen, *Spiritual Friends: A Methodology of Soul Care and Spiritual Direction* (Winona Lake, IN: BMH Books, 2007).

Journey One: *Sustaining Faith—Preserving Trust in the Midst of Doubt (2 Sam. 13:19–21)*

Recall what Nate said to me right after Ashley shared her story with me. "Pastor Bob, can you help? Does the Bible offer any hope for my wife?" How would you be tempted to respond at this point? That's right: with answers—a litany of biblical verses and scriptural principles. Certainly there is a time for interactions that involve scriptural exploration and spiritual conversations. But what does Ashley need *now*? To answer that important question, let's consider how *not* to sustain faith and how *to* sustain faith when a person is battling doubts.

How Not *to Sustain Faith in the Midst of Doubt.* First, we need to be sure that we don't victimize the victim with more voicelessness. Listen again to Tamar's story. "Tamar put ashes on her head and tore the ornamented robe she was wearing. She put her hand on her head and went away, weeping aloud as she went. Her brother Absalom said to her, 'Has that Amnon, your brother, been with you? Be quiet now, my sister; he is your brother'" (13:19–20).

Here is a classic lesson in how *not* to provide soul care. Absalom says, "Be quiet, hold your peace." He's literally telling Tamar to ignore it, to dismiss it, to take no notice of it, and to *not* talk about it! Unfortunately, this whole text is filled with men who will not listen to Tamar. Amnon refuses to listen to her. Absalom won't listen to her. David, her own father, doesn't listen to her—he's furious but inattentive (13:21).

One of the temptations we have as Bible-believing Christians is to race in and tell God's story before we've taken the time to listen to our suffering friend's story. We earn the right to interact about God's eternal story by first listening to our friend's earthly story.

Second, we need to be sure we don't victimize the victim by encouraging more denial. Absalom also tells Tamar, "Don't take this thing to heart" (13:20). This *thing*? He can't even name it! The inspired author named it—rape! Don't take it to *heart*? Where else would she take it? As if the core of Tamar's being can dismiss such degrading abuse. First Absalom says, "Hold your peace. Don't say a word." Then he follows up with, "Stuff it!" Of course, *he's* not stuffing it. He's plotting revenge—murder!

I was moved to tears when Nate humbly and sincerely confessed to Ashley the subtle and not-so-subtle ways he communicated to her, "Be voiceless; remain in denial." While he had not said these phrases, Nate realized that he had communicated things like, "Time heals all wounds." "The past is the past." "Get on with life." "Leave well enough alone." "Don't mess with and pick at the scab, just cope with it."

How to Sustain Faith in the Midst of Doubt. Together, Nate and I began to listen, really listen, to Ashley's soul. We entered the battle for her soul; we entered the black hole of her soul with her. We did so first through compassionate listening. This was also what Tamar was silently screaming for. By putting ashes on her head and weeping aloud, Tamar was doing exactly what a healthy Israelite was supposed to do when they were violated. She was publicly lamenting. The word used for "crying" means to cry aloud from great sorrow while imploring others to help. But no one listened.

Nate was committed to ensuring that Ashley would not be left alone—isolated and desolate—the way Tamar was. He chose to *give her back her voice.* Together Nate and I listened not just for information, but for identification (Rom. 12:15; 2 Cor. 1:3–7). We engaged in incarnational listening (Heb. 2:14–18; 4:14–16). We listened to her words, her tears, her actions, and her emotions. We listened to Ashley's fears, depression, and people-pleasing perfectionism.

Several weeks into our counseling, Ashley described the impact this was having on her. "I really wondered if I could ever open up to anyone about this. I wondered if I could ever trust anyone again—to be safe . . ." Then she stopped talking, stood up, and embraced Nate with a deeply meaningful hug of gratitude.

Ashley not only needed compassionate listening, she longed for empathetic involvement. Tamar desperately needed the same. She received it only from the inspired narrator, who tells us that after Absalom's "counsel," "Tamar lived in her brother Absalom's house, a desolate woman" (13:20). This same word *desolate* is used in Lamentations 1:16 and 3:11 for those who are destroyed by their enemies and those who are torn to pieces by animals.

As Nate listened to Ashley share her soul about her loss of faith, hope, peace, and love, he wept with his wife. As he entered her soul and saw her heart bolted shut, her dreams dashed, her eyes downcast, and her robes torn, Nate was angry *on behalf of* his wife. Through Nate's empathy, Ashley was able to experience the truth that *shared sorrow is endurable sorrow.* No, it doesn't magically erase the agony, but it does supernaturally draw a line in the sand of denial and retreat. Through Nate's empathy, Ashley was also *given permission to grieve.* He communicated that *it is normal to hurt—to ache.* He wept for his wife so that she was freed to weep for herself.

Nate and I engaged with Ashley in a third relational connection—we helped to stretch her back to God. Ponder the relational process so far. By listening, we helped Ashley to *embrace her loss.* Through empathy, we *embraced Ashley in her loss.* Now, through stretching Ashley to God, we helped her to *embrace God and be embraced by God in her loss.*

Isn't that exactly what is needed if the damage of sexual abuse begins with a loss of trust? Consider Tamar again. Have you noticed what is missing in 2 Samuel? *God is missing.* He's missing from the lips of Amnon, Jonadab, David, and Absalom. No male in this text is consciously living *coram Deo*. No one is helping Tamar to live face-to-face with God in her suffering. No one is helping her to face her pain and her doubts, to explore her feelings about God and God's compassion for her.

David—a man after God's own heart, who penned so many *coram Deo* lament psalms—could have mentored his daughter in the composition of songs and psalms of lament. Lament psalms enable the suffering to face the reality that *life is bad—evil, horrible*—while clinging to the reality that *God is good—gracious and compassionate*.

In addition to Ashley writing and sharing lament psalms, we engaged in spiritual conversations where I asked Ashley to share her thoughts about questions such as the following:

- As you read Tamar's story, what is similar and different in what happened to her compared to what you experienced? What is similar and different in how she responded in her soul compared to your soul's response? What is similar and different in how others responded to her and to you?
- If you painted a picture of God as you sense him right now, what would you paint?
- As you've gone through this, what thoughts or feelings have you had about or toward God?
- What doubts, if any, about God's goodness and care have you struggled with? How have you handled them?
- If you were to write a Psalm 13 or Psalm 88 (a psalm of lament), how would it sound?

The Sustaining Word Picture: A Courageous Friend Who Enters the Black Hole. We can capture what Ashley needed in the sustaining process with a word picture: a courageous friend who enters the black hole. If the door of Ashley's heart was bolted shut, then she needed trustworthy people to earn the right to be invited in. Nate and I did not overpower her by breaking in and knocking the door down. We sought to offer her small tastes of grace and goodness—not to point to ourselves, but eventually to point Ashley back to the Son whose light could shine into the darkness of her black hole.

Journey Two: Healing Hope—Clinging to the Goodness of God in the Midst of the Badness of Life (2 Sam. 13:19–20; Gen. 45:5–8; 50:19–20; Hab. 3:17–19)

As Ashley, Nate, and I journeyed together, Ashley was increasingly moving from denial to reality. She was also at the place where she could lament to God—she trusted God enough to share the fine china of her soul with him. However, as Ashley looked at that fine china, it was still in a million shattered pieces. While she was developing the faith and trust to face God face-to-face, Ashley still needed hope that God's goodness could mend and heal the fine china of her heart. Ashley felt powerless, and she needed to know that God was actively at work through his affectionate sovereignty, encouraging and empowering her to be God's poem, his workmanship (Eph. 2:10).

Tamar longed for such hope. Kiel and Delitzsch, in their commentary on this passage, describe Tamar's desolation in 13:20. She was "indeed desolate, as one laid waste, with the joy of her life hopelessly destroyed."[9] An empty shell of her former self, Tamar's hope was shattered. She felt as though from this day forward she would experience only solitude and sorrow. When Ashley and I interacted about this verse, Ashley noted, "I can relate. For me, it has been like the porch light is on, but there's no one home. And . . . sometimes . . . that porch light is out, too . . ."

Explore How God Weaves Good Out of Evil. In the one-another ministry of sustaining and healing, I like to envision

9. Keil and Delitzsch, *Commentary*, 400.

two pivot feet. With one foot we always pivot into the earthly story of our suffering spiritual friend. With the other foot we always pivot with our spiritual friend to God's eternal story of hope. Having earned the right to explore God's story by listening compassionately to Ashley's story, we began to explore how God weaves good out of evil. Because 2 Samuel 13 in itself offers only glimpses of hope, Ashley, Nate, and I explored other passages together. In particular, we interacted about Joseph's story in Genesis 45:5–8 and 50:19–20. Neither passage at all minimizes the sins committed against Joseph. However, both passages highlight God's affectionate sovereignty in turning into good what Joseph's brothers intended for evil.

The particular word for "intended" in Genesis 50:20 was used in the Hebrew language for weaving together a tapestry and interpenetrating fabric to fashion a robe—perhaps even Joseph's coat of many colors. The Old Testament also used the word in a negative metaphorical sense to suggest a malicious plot or cruel scheme. Other times the word is used symbolically to picture the creation of some new and beautiful purpose or result through the weaving together of seemingly haphazard or even malicious events.

"Life is bad," Joseph admits. "You *intended* to spoil or ruin something wonderful." "God is good," Joseph insists. "God wove good out of evil—*intending* to create amazing beauty from seemingly worthless ashes."

We didn't wave this passage over Ashley like a magic wand. Instead, with this passage and many others, we talked, cried, discussed, explored, probed, wondered, and applied. For Ashley, it *began* the process of, as she worded it, "helping me to see that not all power is evil—and that God holds his power for good and beautiful purposes."

Explore How God Empowers Us: When We Are Weak, Then We Are Strong. We also learned together the truth that every victim needs to learn—God not only *holds* his power for good; he *shares* his power for good. Habakkuk 3:17–19 was one of the passages we examined together.

> Though the fig tree does not bud and there are no grapes on the vines, though the olive crop fails and the fields produce no food, though there are no sheep in the pen and no cattle in the stalls, yet I will rejoice in the LORD, I will be joyful in God my Savior. The Sovereign LORD is my strength; he makes my feet like the feet of a deer, he enables me to go on the heights.

This passage helped us to make the biblical connection between hope and empowerment. Realistically facing his current situation, Habakkuk found hope as he looked to his *future with God*. And it was that future hope that empowered Habakkuk to jump for joy and to find strength in God's affectionate sovereignty.

As Ashley put it, "I've been living with 'fake power.' I fake everything! I pretend to serve out of joy, but it's really out of fear. But now, trusting God's good heart once again, my eyes can start to envision a new future, a better future. So now, when I serve Nate or the twins or folks at church, it's coming from a different place with a different motive. I feel a 'soft strength' to love others for Christ again."

It was in this context of God empowering us through hope that Ashley noticed something about 2 Samuel 13 that I had never seen. "Pastor Bob, last week you mentioned that Amnon not only took Tamar's voice away, he also took her name away by calling her 'this thing' (13:17). Well, two verses later, *God gave her back her name!* Verse 19 begins, 'Tamar.' God doesn't share his power as if it's an impersonal force. God *who is the Almighty shares himself with me*—and in the process he's *given me my name back—Ashley!*"

The Healing Word Picture: A Champion Who Celebrates the Resurrection. We can capture what Ashley needed in the healing process with a word picture: a champion who celebrates the resurrection. If life had killed the dreams Ashley dreamed, then she needed hope-giving encouragers to point her to Christ and his resurrection power. She needed people like Nate and me to journey with her to the empty tomb and then celebrate her Savior rolling away the stone from the dead dreams in her life.

Journey Three: Reconciling Peace—Receiving Christ's Grace in the Midst of Our Disgrace (2 Sam. 13:12–13, 20–22; Rom. 5:20)

In ministering to Ashley, so far our focus has been on *applying the gospel to her suffering.* In doing so, we have been following the biblical route traced out in church history—applying the comfort of the cross to the evils people have suffered.

Throughout the Bible and church history, the gospel of Christ's grace has also, of course, been applied to the sins we have committed. In working with someone like Ashley who has been sinned against, we need to ask the question, What is a grace-based response to those who have abused you? As we shall see, this is no shallow and unrealistic "forgive and forget." Yes, forgiveness—but with bold love, like we see in Tamar's courageous confrontation of Amnon (13:12–13).

There is another sin-related area of focus in the Bible and biblical counseling: the *potential sinful response to having been sinfully abused.* Please think carefully with me on this matter. God calls upon us to do the most difficult and delicate of spiritual surgery. We must understand and communicate that the abuse victim did *not* sin in being abused. The abuse victim did *not* sin in feeling emotional pain. As with the man born blind in John 9 and with Job, suffering is often not related to or caused by any personal sin, but due to living in a fallen world.

However, because we are not yet glorified and not yet perfect, and because we still battle against the world, the flesh, and the devil, the abuse victim potentially has become engaged in sinful reactions to life, to God, to self, and to others in response to her or his abuse. Which of us, when sinned against, can claim a perfect, consistent, Christlike response at all times?

In Romans 5:20, Paul informs us that where sin abounds, grace superabounds. We now examine how to apply that gospel truth to the abhorrent sin of sexual abuse. What does God's amazing grace look like when applied by the abuse victim to the abuser? What does God's wonderful grace look like when applied to the abuse victim's own responses to the abuse?

Overwhelming Sin with Grace by Taking Sin Seriously. Tamar's story ends with disgrace, not grace. "And Tamar lived in her brother Absalom's house, a desolate woman. When King David heard all this, he was furious. Absalom never said a word to Amnon, either good or bad; he hated Amnon because he had disgraced his sister Tamar" (13:20–22). Tamar—desolate and disgraced. David—furious, but inactive. Absalom—bitter and vengeful. Everyone in this story is *overwhelmed by sin*. We must never minimize sin, but we must always realize how minuscule sin is when compared with God's grace. The enormity of sin is wildly overwhelmed by the infinite grace of God.

One of the first ways we overwhelm sin with grace is by not being afraid to call the abuse what it is: evil, sinful, wicked, and foolish. The only person who does so in this text is Tamar. " 'Don't, my brother!' she said to him. 'Don't force me. Such a thing should not be done in Israel! Don't do this wicked thing. What about me? Where could I get rid of my disgrace? And what about you? You would be like one of the wicked fools in Israel' " (13:12–13).

We must join the victim of sexual abuse by calling the abuse wicked, evil, folly, despicable—totally apart from the holiness and love of God. This passage cries out for someone, David in particular, to have said to his precious daughter, "What was done to you was vile. It was evil. It was sin. Justice will be done. As I am commanded in Leviticus, I will cut Amnon off from our people. Firstborn or not, he will pay the price for his sin against you." Sexual abuse victims need to hear us express our righteous anger over the evil that was done to them.

Overwhelming Sin with Grace by Taking the Sinful Abuse Seriously. We also overwhelm sin with grace by taking the sinful abuse seriously. There are many detailed, person-specific applications to this principle—far more than we could adequately outline in this brief booklet. But two overriding principles stand out. First, the abused person needs help to work through the forgiveness process. This never means forgetting. It never means minimizing. It never means excusing. What it does mean is a long, careful, individualized process of forgiving others as we have been forgiven in Christ (Eph. 4:32).

As difficult as this was for Ashley, she came to realize that harboring bitterness was both unlike Christ and unhelpful to her growth in Christ. Ashley was "freed" to forgive only after she was "freed" to name her abuse evil. And she was empowered to forgive only as she reflected on Christ's amazing grace in her life.

Second, through bold love the abused person needs strength and wisdom to *seek justice and not vengeance.* For the protection of others, the abuser needs to be confronted. For the benefit of the abuser, the abuser needs to be confronted. Again, this is a long, careful, and person-specific process. And it is one in which the victim must have available the full resources of the body of Christ. Depending upon the specifics of the abuse, decisions need to be made, plans discussed, and support provided regarding (1) contacting the appropriate authorities, (2) contacting and confronting the abuser, (3) contacting and confronting those who were complicit in the abuse (either by not believing the abuse victim or by knowing of the abuse and not protecting the abuse victim), and (4) initiating church discipline with the abuser.[10]

Overwhelming Sin with Grace by Defeating the Lie of "False Guilt." Having briefly outlined confronting the sin related to the abuser, we now focus on addressing possible sin-related issues connected with the person who was abused. First, we need to defeat the satanic lie of "false guilt" or what Paul calls "worldly sorrow" (2 Cor. 7:10). Satan and the sexual abuser will both attempt to make the abuse victim feel guilty for the abuse. With Ashley, I sought to help her discern between true guilt over any sinful response to her abuse (see the next main point) and false guilt or worldly shame over her abuse (see 2 Cor. 7:8–13). Ashley was able to see that as a child she was powerless to stop the abuse, that she was not responsible for the abuse, and that she was the innocent victim. She was able to see that her suffering, pain, and sorrow over the abuse were not sin.

Overwhelming Sin with Grace by Exploring Possible Sinful Response to Sinful Abuse. Now we embark on the most delicate spiritual surgery. While the abuse victim did not sin in being abused, because we are all sinners the abuse victim potentially has sinned in the way she or he has related to God, others, and self as a result of the abuse.

When my journey with Ashley arrived at this point, the waters became rough initially. We had to carefully sort through the difference between being responsible for the abuse and being responsible for her *response to the abuse.* Because Ashley, Nate, and I had built a trusting and supportive relationship, we were able to ride this tide of understandable resistance.

10. For additional wisdom principles for confronting an abuser, see Justin and Lindsey Holcomb, "Confronting an Abuser," Biblical Counseling Coalition, August 29, 2012, http://biblicalcounselingcoalition.org/resources/confronting-an-abuser.

Because of her humble, godly heart, Ashley was able to see and repent of the fallen agenda she had developed in response to her abuse. As she said it in prayer,

> Father, please forgive me for turning to myself instead of to you. I've been living to make my life work without you. Everyone thinks you and I are so close. What they don't know is how I play "the good Christian girl," but inside I've been as far away from you as the prodigal was. I've found so many ways to not need you—to deny the truth that you are indispensable. My works-based self-righteousness is filthy rags. I've trusted in my "good girl" ways, and not in your good grace. I've shut myself off from you, and this has left me empty of resources so that I've closed myself off to Nate and the twins. Father, forgive me. Cleanse me. Empower me to live as your dearly loved daughter. I humbly receive your gracious forgiveness. Thank you for running to me, throwing your arms around me, and celebrating with me my return home to your loving heart . . .

Ashley personalized the truth that *it's horrible to sin, but wonderful to be forgiven.* She personalized the wise counsel that says, "for every one look at your sins, take ten looks at Christ."

The Reconciling Word Picture: A Christ-focused Dispenser of Grace. We can capture what Ashley needs in the reconciling process with a word picture: a Christ-focused dispenser of grace. If loss of peace caused Ashley to live with downcast eyes, always looking down and moving away from God and others, then she needed peace-giving soul physicians to point her to Christ's reconciling grace. She needed Nate and me to journey with her back to God's good and gracious heart. Only grace—Christ's grace—had the power to transport Ashley from alienation from God to reconciliation, from separation from others to connection, from dis-integration with her own self to shalom integration and wholeness.

Journey Four: Guiding Love—Offering Beauty in the Midst of Ashes (2 Sam. 13:19; Isa. 61:1–3)

Recall how Tamar and Ashley both felt used and useless. Remember also how historical Christian guiding emphasizes that *it's supernatural to mature—to love like Christ.* In the guiding process, sexual abuse victims move from being used and feeling useless to being loved by Christ and empowered for useful, meaningful, loving service for him. The goal of sexual abuse "recovery" is not only personal *healing*, but ultimately it is personal *maturity*—growth in Christlikeness.

In 2 Samuel 13:19, Tamar rips her robe and pours ashes on her head—a common cultural symbol for mourning. When I pastored a church in Ohio, I equipped two women to launch and lead a sexual abuse recovery group. They chose the name Beauty for Ashes, taking it from 13:19 and from God's comforting words to Israel in Isaiah 61:1–3.

> The Spirit of the Sovereign LORD is on me, because the LORD has anointed me to preach good news to the poor. He has sent me to bind up the brokenhearted, to proclaim freedom for the captives and release from darkness for the prisoners, to proclaim the year of the LORD's favor and the day of vengeance of our God, to comfort all who mourn, and provide for those who grieve in Zion—to bestow on them a crown of beauty instead of ashes, the oil of gladness instead of mourning, and a garment of praise instead of a spirit of despair. They will be called oaks of righteousness, a planting of the LORD for the display of his splendor.

Notice in this passage that this beauty is not only the return of personal beauty and wholeness, but also beauty shared—loving ministry to others for God's glory.

Encouraging Beauty for Ashes by Envisioning the Beauty of the Soul. We first offer beauty for ashes by envisioning the beauty of the soul. Yes, Ashley was victimized by sexual abuse, but "sexual abuse victim" does not capture the core of her soul. "Beloved and loving daughter of the King" begins to capture the core of Ashley's identity in Christ. When I counseled Ashley I prayed that God would show me the uniqueness of her soul and the unique gifts he had planted within her.

I wonder how the sordid story of Tamar might have ended had David offered eyes of grace to his daughter. What if he had taken her into his house? What if he had looked his daughter in the eyes and said, "I love you, sweetheart. You will always be my precious princess. I am so sorry for Amnon's wicked sin against you. What he did to you is evil, but God is good and gracious. As he has forgiven me in my sin, so he accepts you in your suffering. May my love for you and my arms around you be a small taste of the love your heavenly Father has for you."

Then I imagine David saying, "Come with me!" Hand in hand they stroll to an enormous closet. David flings open the doors, revealing richly ornamented robes for the virgin daughters of the king. "But Father," Tamar protests, "I can't. For I am no longer pure." David responds, "Hush, my sweet child. All is cleansed. In the eyes of the king of Israel and in the eyes of the King of Kings, you are whiter than snow." Tamar then selects a beautiful, feminine, purple robe with white lace. Dignity restored, she becomes renowned throughout the ancient Near East as a woman of gentle grace. If only her father the king had envisioned the beauty of her soul, the world could have rejoiced that *grace makes a rape victim a spiritual virgin*.

Encouraging Beauty for Ashes by Enlightening Abuse Victims to Wisdom Responses. Picture the fruit the gospel has produced thus far. Ashley's faith has been restored as she trusted God in the midst of the doubts that life threw at her. Ashley's hope has been restored as she clung to the goodness of God in the midst of the evil that life threw at her. Ashley's peace has been restored as she received Christ's grace in the midst of the disgrace in this fallen world. Now, through Christ, Ashley's love—her redeemed capacity to love others like Christ—has been restored as she offers beauty to others in the midst of the ashes of life.

Biblical counseling doesn't stop at the counselee or at the door to the counseling office. The real "grace work" of biblical counseling begins when the counselee leaves the counseling office and lives 24/7 in the "real world." As Ashley, Nate, and I worked together, we focused on situation-specific and Ashley-specific biblical wisdom for questions like the following:

- What does renewed and empowered faith and trust look like for you, Ashley, with God, with Nate, with your boys, and with ministry to others?
- What does renewed and empowered hope and joy look like for you, Ashley, with God, with Nate, with your boys, and with ministry to others?
- What does renewed and empowered peace and shalom look like for you, Ashley, with God, with Nate, with your boys, and with ministry to others?
- What does renewed and empowered love and meaningful service look like for you, Ashley, with God, with Nate, with your boys, and with ministry to others?

As Ashley put on the King's robes, she stirred up the gift of God within her. In the specifics of her daily life and relationships, she fanned into flame the faith, hope, peace, and love placed within her regenerated soul.

The Guiding Word Picture: A Coach Who Trains the Heart. We can capture what Ashley needed in the guiding process with a word picture: a coach who trains the heart. If loss of love caused Ashley to tear the robes of the King's daughter, then she needed caring people with spiritual eyes to help her envision who she was in Christ and tap into Christ's resurrection power. She needed Nate and me to journey with her down the gospel path of beauty for ashes—meaningful, loving ministry to others for Christ's glory.

During our final formal counseling meeting, Nate surprised Ashley with a beautiful wood plaque. The wording wove together Isaiah 61:1–3 and the meaning of Ashley's name. It especially highlighted the wording in 61:3, "They will be called oaks of righteousness, a planting of the LORD for the display of his splendor." Ashley's name is derived from a surname based on the Old English word for ash wood, or "lives in the ash tree grove." Nate worded it,

Ashley
One Who Is a Tree Planted by the Streams of Living Water
An Ash Tree Oak of Righteousness
Planted and Nourished by the LORD for the Display of His Splendor

Ashley wept. "I have never liked my name. It seemed so plain—like me. Now I *love* my name! I love my God-given, Christ-redeemed purpose!"

KEEP CLINGING TO CHRIST

Dear reader, never forget who you are in Christ. You are the King's daughter or son. You are God's workmanship, his epic poem, his opus, his masterpiece. All the evil you have ever suffered, God in Christ has been weaving together for good— for beauty, for splendor. Continue to live your life based upon your belief in God's mission statement: *"I Am Indispensable."* Continue to journey down life's path with God's prescription for our disgrace—grace.

Applying the Gospel to Daily Life

1. **God's Mission Statement:** *"I Am Indispensable."* In what specific ways can your life communicate your belief in and surrender to God's mission statement?

2. **The Damage of Loss of Trust: The Attempted Destruction of Faith.** How has your openness to trust in God and connection with others been impacted by the abuse you suffered? How does your response to your abuse contrast and compare with Tamar's response in 2 Samuel 13:1–12? With Ashley's response?

3. **The Damage of Powerlessness: The Attempted Destruction of Hope.** How has your ability to dream, hope, long, want, and choose been affected by the abuse you suffered? How does your response to your abuse contrast and compare with Tamar's response in 2 Samuel 13:2, 11–14? With Ashley's response?

4. **The Damage of Shame: The Attempted Destruction of Peace.** In response to your abuse, in what ways have you struggled with shame, self-contempt, feelings of rejection and disgrace, guilt, and difficulties connecting deeply? How does your response to your abuse contrast and compare with Tamar's response in 2 Samuel 13:13–17? With Ashley's response?

5. **The Damage of Being Used and Feeling Useless: The Attempted Destruction of Love.** In response to your abuse, in what ways have you struggled with feelings of worthlessness and lovelessness? How does your response to your abuse contrast and compare with Tamar's response in 2 Samuel 13:14–20? With Ashley's response?

6. **Sustaining Faith: Preserving Trust.** Who has truly entered the battle for your soul—entered the black hole with you? How has their presence impacted you? In what

ways are you embracing God again and experiencing the embrace of God?

7. **Healing Hope: Clinging to the Goodness of God.** In what ways are you beginning to see God weave good out of the evil of your abuse? In your weakness, how are you finding and relying upon God's strength? How are you finding God?

8. **Reconciling Peace: Receiving Christ's Grace.** Through Christ, how have you been overwhelming sin with grace by taking sin seriously? By taking the sinful abuse seriously? By defeating the lie of "false guilt"? By exploring possible sinful responses to the sinful abuse?

9. **Guiding Love: Offering Beauty for Ashes.** What does renewed and empowered faith and trust look like for you? Renewed and empowered hope and joy? Renewed and empowered peace and shalom? Renewed and empowered love and meaningful service?

10. **Grace: God's Prescription for Our Disgrace.** Through Christ's grace, how will you continue to journey down life's path with God's prescription for your disgrace—grace? Through grace, how will your life be God's masterpiece displaying the splendor of Christ's grace?

MORE HELP FOR VICTIMS OF ABUSE
FROM P&R PUBLISHING

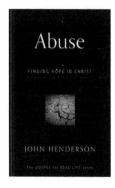

What does the gospel have to say when we are victims of evil? John Henderson provides Psalm 22 as a framework for responding to abuse and understanding how God comforts the afflicted through his Word, bringing it to bear in the life of a couple deeply affected by childhood sexual abuse. Their example shows the beauty and light of the gospel, and how it brings hope and perspective in the darkest of our circumstances.

"With the heart of a pastor, John Henderson helps us to see how Scripture really does make a difference in life's most difficult hurts, pains, and sorrows."
—**Deepak Reju,** Associate Pastor, Capitol Hill Baptist Church, Washington, D.C.

Domestic Abuse teaches that violent people have much in common with others. Once you know how to deal with your own anger, you can help others who struggle with violence.

RESOURCES FOR CHANGING LIVES SERIES FROM P&R

How could God allow this to happen to me? I'm angry with him, but I don't know if I'm "supposed" to be angry!

Is it okay to be angry with God? If we are angry, should we hold it inside or voice our feelings outright?

Jones writes that we should not take a "grin and bear it" approach to our anger, nor should we rashly vent our emotions to God. Instead, we need to humbly bring him our struggles, doubts, and questions. We must learn to be transparent in God's presence, think biblically, and act obediently.

OTHER BOOKLETS IN THE SERIES INCLUDE:

Anger, David Powlison

Depression, Edward T. Welch

God's Love, David Powlison

Forgiveness, Robert D. Jones

Homosexuality, Edward T. Welch

Just One More, Edward T. Welch

Pornography, David Powlison

Suffering, Paul David Tripp

Suicide, Jeffrey S. Black

Thankfulness, Susan Lutz

Why Me?, David Powlison

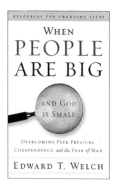

"Need people less. Love people more. That's the author's challenge. . . . He's talking about a tendency to hold other people in awe, to be controlled and mastered by them, to depend on them for what God alone can give. . . . [Welch] proposes an antidote: the fear of God . . . the believer's response to God's power, majesty and not least his mercy."
  —*Dallas Morning News*

"Refreshingly biblical . . . brimming with helpful, readable, practical insight."
  —**John MacArthur,** president of The Master's College and Seminary

"Ed Welch is a good physician of the soul. This book is enlightening, convicting, and encouraging. I highly recommend it."
  —**Jerry Bridges,** author of *Trusting God*